*Moving into the Space
Cleared by Our Mothers*

By the same author

'A Noise from the Woodshed'
(Onlywomen Press, 1989)
'Kindling'
(Onlywomen Press, 1982)

MARY DORCEY

Moving into the Space Cleared by Our Mothers

SALMON  POETRY

Acknowledgements are due to the following anthologies and journals
in which some of these poems first appeared:
'New Angles', Oxford University Press; 'Bread and Roses',Virago Press,
'In the Pink', The Women's Press, 'Beautiful Barbarians', Onlywomen
Press, 'Feminism in Ireland', Pergamon Press, 'Naming the Waves',
Virago Press, 'Erotica – Writing by Women', Pandora Press, 'Ain't I a
Woman?', Virago Press, 'New Irish Writing', Oklahoma University Press,
'The Spare Rib Health Book', Pandora Press, Plexus; Off Our Backs;
Wicca; Spare Rib; Irish Women's Diary; W.E.A. Journal; Fan.

'Kindling' (Onlywomen Press, 1982)

Some of these poems have been performed on stage.

First published in 1991 by
Salmon Publishing, Bridge Mills, Galway.
This edition 1994 by Salmon Publishing Limited,
A division of Poolbeg Enterprises Ltd,
Knocksedan House,
123 Baldoyle Industrial Estate,
Dublin 13, Ireland

ISBN 1 897648 25 1

Cover illustration by Reiltín Murphy
Back cover photograph by Joe Geoghegan
Cover design by Poolbeg Group Services Ltd
Typesetting and Design by Johan Hofsteenge
Printed by Colour Books, Baldoyle Industrial Estate, Dublin 13

for my mother

The Publishers gratefully acknowledge the support of

The Arts Council / An Chomhairle Ealaíon.

Contents

I

II

From 'Kindling'

I

In the City of Boston

I have seen mad women in my time,
I have seen them waiting row on row,
I have seen the stripped flesh,
the abandoned eye,
I have seen the frothing mouth
and heard the cries,
I have seen mad women in my time
- I have never seen them mad enough.

In the city of Boston I once saw a woman
and she was mad - as mad as they come
(and oh do they come, mad women,
as often as the rest?)
She walked the street in broad daylight,
neat as a pin - a lady no doubt
in blue coat, blue hat, blue purse
blue shoes - the only note
out of place in it all
was her face - the peculiar angle
of her head; thrown back, jaws wide
and a scream so shrill poured out
it lifted the birds from her feet.

Sunshine in an elegant Boston square
choc-o-bloc with the office lot
loosed to eat,
no one turned, no one stared
from their clean cut day,
nobody cared to embarrass the mad.
She strode through that crowd

sealed tight in her mind,
chin high, clutching her bag,
her terrible siren full on.

Mechanical agony guided her step
until she reached the pavement's edge.
There at the crossroads
- an extraordinary thing -
her polished shoes halted,
she lowered her head,
the animal howl died in her throat -
stock still, patient, ordered
she stood
because the traffic light was red.

I have seen mad women in my time,
I have seen them burn
the skin from their breasts,
I have seen them claw a lover's eyes,
I have seen the blade across the bone,
have seen the frothing mouth
and heard the moan -
I have seen the abandoned faces
row on row,
I have seen mad women in my time
- I have never seen us mad enough.

Beginning

She showered and scoured
her skin clear.
Dressed in fresh clothes,
cut her hair
and old friends.
Took up Aikido, Celtic studies and Zen.
Tore up snapshots and letters,
painted all her walls white.
Smiled at each woman she passed
in the street.
And asked nobody home
who might find out
that for months
she still slept
in your blood stained
sheets.

Not Everyone Sees This Night

The first frost
has brought back summer.
Walking in the garden
my feet crack the whitened grass -
the smell is of hay -
just cut.

They ask me
if I'm happy here -
they ask
as if used to answers.

The sky is luminous and vast
more blue than day;
it cannot hold its stars -
they spill wide and down
I hear them fall
behind the black mountains.

No one has seen such a moon!

The silence is the loudest thing:
breath roars out -
a milky stream,
and yes -
a moment later
from off stage -
comes the sea.

They ask me
if I'm happy here.

A dog bays to stretch the quiet.
Two miles off
a neighbour's light
goes dark.
The cats forsake the hearth
to roll
spring madness
on the spiked crunch
of earth.

Beneath its slates
the house huddles -
yellow eyes gleaming.
The mallow in blossom
purple at the gate.

Sometimes when I go in
you are asleep -
your bed under the skylight.
Sometimes I do not wake you.

Not everyone sees
this night -
there are others -
here
and elsewhere.

Not everyone
sleepless in these hours,
watching for dawn
regrets its coming.

I pluck the ice cold grass -
a handful
and go indoors.

I hold it to my lips
before I kiss you
so that when I do
your lips -
burn.

First Love

You were tall and beautiful.
You wore your long dark hair
wound about your head,
your neck stood clear and full
as the stem of a vase.
You held my hand in yours
and we walked slowly
talking of small familiar happenings
and of the lost secrets
of your childhood.

It seems it was always autumn then.
The amber trees shook.
We laughed in a wind
that cracked the leaves from black boughs
and sent them scuffling about our feet
for me to trample still and kick
in orange clouds about your face.

We would climb dizzy
to the cliff's edge
and gaze down at a green and purple
sea, the wind howling
in our ears as it tore
the breath from white cheeked waves.
You steadied me
against the wheeling screech
of gulls and I loved to think
that but for your strength
I would tumble to the rocks below

to the fated death
your stories made me dream of.

I do not remember
that I looked in your eyes
or that we ever asked
an open question.
Our thoughts passed
through our blood, it seemed,
and the slightest pressure
of our hands
decided all issues wordlessly.

We watched in silence
by the shore, the cold
spray against our skin;
in mutual need
of the water's fierce, inhuman
company that gave promise
of some future, timeless
refuge from the fixed
anxieties
of our world.
As we made for home

We faced into the wind.
My thighs were grazed
by its ice teeth.
You gathered your coat about me
and I hurried our steps

towards home, fire, and
the comfort of your sweet, strong tea.
We moved bound in step.
You sang songs of Ireland's troubles
and of proud women loved
and lost.
I knew then they set for me
a brilliant stage of characters

Who even now
can seem more vivid
than my own chosen friends.
We walked together
hand in hand.
You were tall and beautiful.
You wore your long dark hair
wound about your head
your neck stood clear and full
as the stem of a vase.
I was young -
you were my mother
and it seems
it was always
autumn then.

White Light

White light   dark inside me
light growing whiter   inside me
growing whiter   inside me
growing dark   inside me   whiter
than white   growing dark inside
though I did not know it
then   and now   why now?

And you were kind to me when?
Kind smiling   tender
my kind   a kiss was a comfort   a prayer
a huddle against darkness   growing
whiter and white light inside.

Was I not kind back
was I not   was I not?
Did I hurt not knowing
did I hurt?
Hurting so much myself.
Hurting we all hurt
all of us together
fighting the darkness
growing whiter.

Love   you called love
love   love   lover
love me   love me   love me.
Is there another?
the old cry
is there another than this cry?

than this one   always
huddling together
darkness growing   love me
love me   love me.

And you did
love
you did by any standards -
you did in your way
love me -
not in my way
not in my way
lover.

Deliberately Personal

Who is the woman
who drove the children to school
made the beds and washed the dishes -
who hoovered the wall to wall carpet -
before slitting her throat at the bathroom mirror?

Who is the man
who drove his favourite niece to the party
in her flowered pink frock -
in her ribbons and bows;
who raped her on the back seat
on the way back -
Why not? he said
look how she was dressed?
and besides -
hadn't she been doing it for years
with her father?

Who are these people -
where do they come from?
What kind of man -
what kind of woman?
Where do they live -
who lives next door to them?
How come none of us
ever knows them?

And how is it;
wherever it happens -
he doesn't belong to us?
How is it he's always
somebody else's
brother, father, husband?

Why is it
whoever she is
she's never more
than a name in the papers -
some vagrant, friendless
unnatural woman?

And who are you
come to that?
All of you
out there
out of the spotlight -
out for a night's entertainment,
smiles upturned so politely;
asking me
why I have to be -
so raw
and deliberately
personal?

Come Close to Me

Come close to me.

Let me feel the heat
the light   the scent of you
near me.
Open your mouths
  shield me
Let me feel the ice
sweetness of your hands
catch fire.
Breath of my breath
bind and loose me
  quicken and still me -
held in your voice
  the blade of your skin
the fall of your thighs

Come close to me.

Trying on for Size

Capsized on the bed
you roll
cane white legs
tapping the air.
You are pulling on your stockings -
easier now this way
than to stand upright and bend.
You are laughing
because I've caught you at it
one of your secret stratagems.

On the beach in summer
years ago,
a birth mark on your calf
shamed you -
when you were young in summer
your limbs long and full
your shoulders broad.
You swam with mighty strokes
out so far
I watched in awe
until your beauty
was a bird or buoy
dancing between waves.

With each new day behind you
you ask
do you remember when...?
and I do -
almost all of it
and more.

25

You were not always good.
You threatened with a wooden spoon,
cursed me when there was no one else to curse.
At sea in your kitchen
you did not counsel or console,
you turned your eyes from trouble
having known too much of it
uncomforted yourself.

Going down the stairs now
behind your anxious, baby steps
I want to pick you up and carry you
or launch you down the banister
as you did me
in this house
when we were children together.

But you must take every step first
along this passage
we daughters follow after
each one of us
moving into the space
cleared by our mothers.

And with what fine nerve,
what unthanked grace,
you confront this last world
you will discover before me.

I see your shy, jaunty smile
at the mirror -
see you say
what do you think?
As if death
were a foolish, extravagant hat
you were trying on for size.

I Will Leave This Place

I will leave this place,
and go somewhere
you are not known.
Days might pass,
without hearing your name.

Taking the Boat

The granite piers of the harbour
stretch towards me across a still sea
Gulls fly out from our side like
streamers and dip to harass small
waves scattered by the bows.
But tonight there is nothing rosy
in this vision but the ruddy
smooth clouds that have blossomed
above the Dublin hills.
This time I have come back
before memory could daze sense or
cast its rainbow across these waters.

In the second class lounge, eyes assume
the fixed glaze requisite for home.
The one defence of men who refuse
to commit themselves to life but
watch it sceptical from barstools as if
it could be bought off forever
with rounds of stout.
On shore the squat roofs huddle
about a high church spire, pink and
white bunting on seafront hotels marshal
a faded festivity, old men and women stroll
the promenade, this arrival the one event

Of their evening. On deck we watch
the land draw in as if waiting the
recommencement of an atavistic curse.
Beside me a neighbour's lips move silently
driven by involuntary prayer. The
rain begins to fall in slow fat drops.
No one has thought to bring raincoat
or umbrella. So we shuffle onto land
heads bowed beneath our coats -
'Ah sure, there'll be a train now soon
enough!' And looking up, I see
the burnished sky of sunset
has gone out
above the hills.

Gaining Health by a Gradual Process of Elimination

Nothing much I can do -
unless you're prepared to give up -
ancient familiar words
of nuns, parents and priests.
The doctor pronounces them now
his little knife poised.

Nothing much I can do
unless you give up -
and I did,
everyone of them,
one by one,
stripped until my bones shone.

What else is left?
Sipping brandy,
wrapped in furs,
smiling my sister asks
- meat, men, cigarettes, booze,
anything else?

Oh yes,
one thing there was
and now its come round,
strange that it took them so long,
the one thing left unnoticed -
you.

Songs of Peace

for a young woman marching against war in the streets of Dublin

Women in the streets again,
hundreds in the streets again,
marching, holding hands,
singing frail songs against
death and destruction.
We don't want to die in your nuclear war.
At every barrier we stand and chant
into the visored eyes,
when they link arms against us we call
nuclear bombs kill gardai too.

We have turned full circle
to the sixties and hippies
scattering flowers for peace.
Nuns have joined us now -
changed their habits for tracksuits,
white masks on their faces
they bear black coffins
for sisters killed by soldiers.
We shall overcome, they sing.
Fifteen years ago I did not ask,

What or when or whom?
And you tell me with pride
you will stay all night in the park,
in the wet and the dirt and the dark,
laying your body down

between life and their weapons.
And yet you confide, with the
injured eyes of a child
refused, that when they arrested
you at the gate,

They shoved and taunted and abused.
And I have been told
that the women at Greenham wept
when they woke to find missiles
brought in while they slept,
as though patient protest
might establish a claim
to codes of war and fair warning.
And I wish you were right,
I wish it were true that

If women enough would gather,
women enough, would leave
husbands and children and sing,
laying their bodies down in the muck.
Yet how often before
have we offered our flesh, in hope,
in barter, in supplication?
And who will it please, if they come
for us, to find this time
we have made our own camps

Unarmed in the dirt and dark?
And I wish you were right
that songs and kisses could do,
hold back bullet and bomb,
loose power, reclaim the night.
But soldiers have always liked songs of peace,
and women have sung them to war before this.
And on return they have paid their respects,
have buried us bravely, buried us well,
with love and flowers and songs of peace.

Return

At last, the train will lurch in,
twenty minutes past the hour, the
dark flesh of the hills, heaved behind -
before us, the narrowing fields,
the layered clouds, drifting
beyond, - lit for some other advent.
And everything will conspire
against me: luggage and children
crowding the aisle. A white haired
woman, home from England,

Awkward with haste, will labour
her case to the door, her floral
print dress, a last check between me
and my first glimpse of you.
And there you are - by the turnstile
I will see you come through, though you
miss me; your brilliant eyes in flight
along the carriage windows.
You will wear your red, linen shirt,
the sleeves turned back and snatched

From the hedgerows as you drove
a swathe of flowers in your arms.
(Such a trail strewn behind us - a trail
of departures and pardons.) And my
blood will betray me - the old response,
I will hesitate, as if there might
still be time to change course,
or simply, not wanting to be caught

waiting for your gaze? The sky
will shift as I step out, a handful

Of sun thrust down on your hair.
On the narrow platform, our hips
will draw close, we will not mind
how they stare - the aggrieved faces
such a fuss -
for a woman!
And in that moment - your laughter,
the heat of your neck at my mouth,
it will all be behind me again,
I swear, as though coming home -
as though for the first time.

Legacy

A scream waits inside me
since my father died,
the tall, loving father
who went off and died
without a word,
leaving mother and sister
and brothers and me.
They screamed when they heard,
the primal scream; my mother
my sister - my little sister,

Two years older than me,
her pale face cracked by it.
We could not all scream.
I held her hand,
my frail, feminine sister,
her father's pride.
I was the brave one, the silent -
only fair,
we each had a favourite parent
and I had kept mine.

I scream now at incongruous
times, little things set me off:
as a ship sails out
and I watch the water scythed
white and bleeding from its bows.

At the movies, when they
lower a coffin down, and
up comes the rattle of the clay.
In the old people's home,
spooning the soup, my aunt's

Chin nodding on its stalk.
I scream when you are tender,
solicitous, your talk
full of love, your eyes
straying over my shoulder.
Oh father, father, father dear
who took off and died
without a word, daddy so
prudent, commanding and wise
who left me here

With this scream inside.
Was it fear to see the mighty
fallen or to learn so soon
that love cannot provide?
Ah no, deeper than this,
I realise, darker than grief
your legacy, when
I wake in my mother's house
on a morning in winter, and up
from the kitchen comes clear

The sound of her singing,
every word off by my heart.
Oh daddy, my grey eyed father,
daddy so wise, loving and prudent,
to one daughter you taught
the dread of betrayal, but guilt
was your parting gift to me.
We each had a favourite parent,
my little sister and I,
and it was not mine that died.

If Only She Had Told You Beforehand

It's not the thing itself
that stinks -
you said,
just that she did it
without any warning.

If she had told you
beforehand
(if the right ever knows
what the left is planning?)
it would have been
different ...

if she had trusted -
confided ...
(if she had known enough to tell
would she have felt enough to do it?)
even hinted ...

if she had taken
the time -
sat you down and
explained the whole story

it would have been easy -
well prepared ...
you might even
have laughed ...

kissed their cheeks -
waved them off
as they climbed
the stairs
to your bed ...

well
maybe not quite ...
flowers
in their hair ...

but it would have been
different -

if only
she had told you
beforehand.

Daughter

And you my daughter
who I will not know -
I feel in mine
your small, hot hand.
I see your green eyes
lighting already
with my mother's far away look,
and the kisses
that might have made you
from my lover's warm, dark lips
smiling from yours -
made for kisses.

My little daughter
what times we shall have -
what talks.
I would hold up the stars
to keep from burning you
quiet the sea
to keep from waking you.
I would eat you for breakfast
all your fat, buttery flesh
thighs and arms
toast and honey.

My little daughter
you will not have the chance
to jail me with your tenderness
grow high and lovely
from my shrinking hide.

We will not now
confront each other
barter, threaten, promise
we will not curse each other
win or lose
my darling
we have no time for that.

I will bequeath you
little -
some words
angry, loving, careful
set down to make a space for you.

I will leave you
flowers and flame
scorched earth, black water
blue skies, laughter
hungry children
women working, loving
fire and ice
bombs and books.

I will leave you
my daughter
this whole wide world
that was not yet
wide enough for me
to bear you into.

First Look

I could more easily
forget
retract
cancel
every word spoken
in and out of anger
than surrender
give back
the moment
the memory
(before any sound
between us
defined
defended)
the first touch
look
lapse
into sense -
your eyes
taking hold of me.

Hands

An old woman is working
in a garden
raking dead leaves
from the earth;

back bent to uncover
the first growth
of a new season.

Will I not see you again?
my blood cannot believe it
- though I have chosen.

You talk too much
- think too much, you said
as I did, and do.
I love
- I loved your hands
that were never still
shaped to their own purpose
by the shaping of things.

Your hands that were not cruel.
The tongue wounds at a slip;
eyes in a glance
or the refusal of it
tear at the heart's root.
But your hands made a silence
wherever they touched,
a stopping place -
the first before love.

The evenings lengthen -
light holds on
for hours in the sky.
Time wipes it all clear
they say, all but
a way of standing
the timbre of a voice.

Thinking of talking -
I wait for night
at a window.

I spread my hands, empty
on the pane -
hands almost still.
I watch an old woman
working -
turning up new soil
in a garden.

The Ordinary Woman

And again you ask me why -
Why don't I write a poem about
The ordinary woman?
Not the extreme, individual case,
But the normal woman, the average woman
The everyday woman?

The woman in the street
The woman in the field
The woman who works in a factory
The woman who works on a farm
The woman who has never heard of a factory
The woman who has never seen a field.

The woman who stays at home
The woman who has no home
The woman who raises children
The woman who can have no children
The woman who has too many children
The woman who wants no children.

The healthy woman   the sick woman
The growing woman   the dying woman
The menstruating woman   the menopausal woman
The married woman   the spinster woman
The woman on the make
The woman on the shelf.

The woman who works in a school
The woman who dropped out of school
The woman who never got into school.
The woman who works as a nurse
The woman who cooks for the nurse
The woman who cleans the kitchen

Where they cook for the nurse.
The woman who works in a shop every day
The woman who shops every day
The woman who shops for food
The woman who shops for clothes, for perfume
The woman who shoplifts

For clothes, for perfume.
The woman who is paid to catch
The woman who does not pay
For clothes   for food.
The career woman   the poetess woman
The mother earth woman   the charwoman

The amazon woman   the society woman
The sportswoman   the little woman
The woman who runs   the woman who walks
The woman who is on the run
The woman who has never walked.
The woman who drives a car

The woman who drives her husband's car.
The pampered woman   the kept woman
The sheltered woman   the battered woman
The victimised woman   the violent woman
The woman nobody wants
The woman who had it coming.

The woman who went sane
The woman who stayed mad
The woman who carries a gun
The woman who is shot by a gun
The woman with too much past
The woman with too little future.

The woman ahead of her times
The woman behind the times
The woman with no time.
The outdated rural woman
The alienated suburban woman
The overcrowded urban woman.

The woman who reads the news
The woman who has never made the news
The woman who starves herself to look right
The woman who starves.
The houseproud woman   the tinker woman
The family woman   the deserted woman

The illegitimate woman   the certified woman
The consumer woman   the alien woman
The emigrant woman   the immigrant woman
The decent woman   the fallen woman
The mother of his children   and
The other woman.

The articulate woman   the illiterate woman
The bluestocking woman   the ignorant woman
The deaf woman   the blind woman
The loud woman   the dumb woman
The big woman   the petite woman
The flatchested woman

The look at those tits woman
The ugly woman   the femme fatale woman
the feminine woman   the masculine woman
The painted woman   the naked woman
The lilywhite and the scarlet woman.
The woman who thinks too much

The woman who never had time to think.
The woman who fights the system
The woman who married the system
The woman who swims against the tide
The woman who swells the tide that drowns
The woman who swims against it.

The woman who sends her sons to kill
The sons of other women.
The woman who sees her daughters
Murdered by the sons of other women.
The woman who is capitalised
The woman who is communised

The woman who is colonised
The woman who is terrorised
The woman who is analysed
The woman who is advertised
The woman who is fertilised
The woman who is sterilised.

The woman who is locked in
The woman who is locked out
The woman in a prison cell
The woman in a convent cell
The woman who keeps her place
The woman who has no place.

The woman who loved her father too much
The woman who loved her mother too much
The woman who hates men
The woman who loves men
The woman who hates women
The woman who loves women.

The natural woman   the perverted woman
The veiled woman   the virgin woman
The celibate woman   the prostitute woman
The jewish woman   the buddhist moslem catholic
Hindu protestant woman
The french woman   the irish woman

The chinese woman   the indian woman
The african woman   the american woman.
The upperclass   upper middle class
Middle class   lower middle class
Upper working class   working class
Lower working class   the no class woman.

The who ever heard of her woman?
The who the hell is she woman?
The who the hell does she think she is woman?
The chaste woman   the frigid woman
The vamp the tramp and the nymphomaniac woman
The wholesome woman   the homely woman

The easy woman   the tight assed woman
The ball breaking   cock teasing
Doesn't know what she's made for woman.
The selfish woman   the martyred woman
The sluttish woman   the fussy woman
The loose woman   the uptight woman

The naive woman   the paranoid woman
The passive woman   the dominant woman
The silly woman   the hard woman
The placid woman   the angry woman
The sober woman   the drunken woman
The silent woman   the screaming woman

Yes, that's it - that's the one
Why don't you write a poem for her -
The ordinary woman?

Love's Labour Lost

She left the party -
with somebody else.
And you had been so good
waiting until two:
her first night off the booze;
you wanted to celebrate -

Congratulate
all that restraint.
But she left the party
sober -
with somebody else.

To Light You to Bed

The pubs were still loud and brilliant
but you had a bus to catch.
We had said everything - that could be said
by friends, and we were sensible.
Through the half-lit streets we walked
somnambulent; ignorant of everyone.
The night was a cord pulled taut
between us, yet we did not touch.

But she knew
and had more courage -
your five year old daughter
impatient beside us
snatched our awkward hands
and clap - she swung them together:
'Here comes a candle to light you to bed'
and - clap -
sang out her latest song:
'Here comes a chopper to chop off your head!'

Repossession

They took out your womb
this year.
You had no use for it.
Every few hours
its memory
bloodies your cheek
as if you were fifty again.

You are stooped and frail
and thin
your fingers swollen
your knees don't work.

You who swung me high -
my chariot -
my tree house.

To think that once
your flesh
was fat and full enough
to feed me
to think you suckled me -
to think I broke from your body
wet and dark -
sleek as a seal's head
breaking water.

As the days draw in
your mind mislays everything
but the past.
Wanting the stairs
you walk into the kitchen.
Time slips through your fingers
you sort old treasures;
guilt and lost chances -
your own mother
who died in a Home
because you had
all of us
children
to think of.

Becalmed at your fireside -
you talk to her
and she talks back -
endlessly sifting
the argument.
Hour by hour
she reclaims you.
She has grown into your lapses -
into your hands
into your walk.

Like mother - like daughter
I say: excuses - justification.

And standing to clear the table
impatient of all this blather
I catch sight of myself
in the mirror -
the gilt-framed glass
that she left you
and oh -
there you are
reflected
already -
fitting new quarters
looking out from
my eyes.

Sea Change

Your thighs your belly -
their sweep and strength -
your breasts so sudden;
nipples budding in my hands,
the sheen of your back
under my palms
your flanks smooth as flame.

Your skin - that inner skin
like silk,
your mouth deepening
full as an orchid
honey on my tongue.

The dizzy lurch and sway -
sea flowers under water;
changing skins with every touch
and then, and again, that voice
- your voice, breaking over me,
opening earth with its call
and rocking the moon in her tide.

Silences

And there is nothing to be said.
One sentence has silenced us.
Your mother dying
And you alone know it.

It is the word that terrifies
you tell us.
She will not hear it,
will not admit its dark force

Into the light of everyday pain.
Unspoken, it cannot take up residence
amid the furniture of her life
cannot look from a mirror

Sit by her bedside, stretch
its hand to open or close
a door. All this her eyes make plain
light with fear

They follow you from chair
to window, plucking at each movement
as if they had power to anchor
her to an unaltered present.

In their mute appeal
you recognise the old demand
to keep truth out of sight and mind.
Eyes skilful as her own

You answer her with silence
Changing the sheets and flowers
as though each day led to another.
And you no longer raise the blinds

But sit quiet in the shadows
knowing as you both must
the reason for your staying,
the best kept truth

Your love of women -
the old secret that binds you here,
that has shaped your hands
for this last work

The love begun with this woman
that now seals her life.
Watching through sleepless nights
in the gloom of old, repeated stories

Your fingers restless at her pillow
And no comfort in knowing
that death is the last word
you will ever fear to tell her.

Therapist

What joy is there?
she asked me
with her cool, unanswering
therapist's eye -
quick to excuse, hesitation
half truth.
Any joy equal to the pain?
I could name none.

Not what you would title
joy.
Nothing large or unsullied
enough for that.
I rifle my brain:
A quietness -
(or something like it
could I offer in defence?)
in crowded places
when our hands touch?
At railway stations
like an old movie
keeping pace with the carriage window?

Breakfast on dark afternoons
the smell of skin
the line of bone,
my mouth remembers
better than my eyes?
Walking six miles
in rain
to finish an argument?
Laughing sometimes.
Making a plan?

Her eye waits -
my own, downcast,
in silence
I shuffle the file:
Not much
to venture
against all this damage,
I have brought
for repair.

Come Quietly or the Neighbours Will Hear

Have you ever made love
with the t.v. on
- to spare the neighbours
landlady lord -
the embarrassment;
the joy undisguised
of two people;
especially women
(imagine the uproar!)
coming together?

Come quietly
or the neighbours will hear.

That year was the worst
an aching winter of it -
small minds and towns
rented rooms and narrow beds,
walled in by other people's
decencies
and at every sitting down
to table,
broadcast at breakfast
dinner and tea
the daily ration
of obscenity.
Have you ever
made love with the t.v. on?

Come quietly
or the neighbours will hear.

On a dark evening
autumn cloths spread for tea,
fires lit.
In the wet gardens
leaves falling
on a dark evening
at last alone
a space, hungry with wanting
waiting, a fire catching
we fell -
skin in firelight burning
fell the long fall
to grace, to the floor.
On a dark evening
night coming softly in the wet gardens.

Come quietly
or the neighbours will hear.

Mouth at my breast
hands ringing in my flesh
when the Angelus rang
from the t.v. screen.
The angel of the lord
declared unto Mary
and she conceived of the Holy Ghost
the earth, the sun and the seas.

Hail Mary   Holy Mary.
Be it done unto me according
to thy word
Hail Mary, and oh -
the sweetness of your breath -
the breath of your sweetness.

Come quietly
or the neighbours will hear.

And the word was made flesh
and dwelt amongst us.
Hands skin mouth thighs
in the bedrock of flesh
sounding,
fields flooded
blood uncoursed.
Blessed art thou
and blessed is the fruit
of thy womb.
Bitter and sweet
earth opens stars collide.
Blessed and sweet,
the fruit
among women
Hail Mary   Holy Mary.

Come quietly
or the neighbours will hear.

When the six o'clock news
struck.
Into the fissures
of mind   and bone
the deadly tide
seeping.
The necessary,
daily litany.
Come quietly or the neighbours
will hear.

She was found
on a park bench backstreet barn
dancehall schoolyard bedroom bar -
found with multiple stab wounds to
thighs breast and abdomen.
Come quietly   come quietly
or the neighbours ...
hands tied behind her back,
no sign of
(mouth bound)
no sign of
sexual assault.

Come softly
or the neighbours will hear.

Your breast and belly,
your thighs,
your hands behind my back
my breath in yours.
No one heard her scream.
Your eyes wide.
Come quietly or the neighbours...
She was found
at the dockside riverbank,
in the upstairs flat
his flat
wearing a loose ...
Your mouth at my ear.

Come quietly
or the neighbours will hear.
Blood on the walls
and sheets,
a loose negligée
in her own flat,
stripped to the waist.
Come quietly, come quietly.
No one heard her scream -
come softly or the neighbours ...
Did you ever make love
with the t.v. on?
- the neighbours heard nothing -
she was always -
no one would have thought -
always a quiet girl.

Stripped to the bone
blood on our thighs
my hands behind your back
come quietly, come,
legs tangled with the sheet
mouth to mouth
voices flung.

Come softly
or the neighbours will hear.

Did you ever make love
with the t.v. on?
to spare the neighbours
landlady lord
her cries in our ears
we came ...
no one heard her scream
her blood on our hands.
Yes -
coming,

Not quietly -
beyond bearing;
in the face of the living
in the teeth of the dying
forgetting the uproar
the outrage -

(imagine -
the joy
undisguised
of two women
- especially
women -)
two women
together -
at last alone
night falling in the wet gardens
on a dark evening
with the t.v.
off.

Die quietly -
die quietly -
or the neighbours will hear.

Snow-in-Summer

April came, then May -
lilac blossom,
cowslip,
snow-in-summer
rampant -
still I woke each morning
with my fists
clenched.

Drunken Truths

She returned,
talking of a new peace -
a life gathered and full,
stripped of the old refuges
of sober lies and drunken truths.
Quiet in the country nights
fasting on poetry and brown rice,
she shares a bed of chastened love
where spiritual subtleties
have replaced the old
crude language of the flesh.

A community of loving couples,
they build together, against
harsh New England winters -
one friend, it seems, still talks too much
and has not yet found her sister
but all things ripen
with time and labour.
She talked to us with earnest eyes
straining through grey smoke
- she would quit for sure
next week, she said -

But meantime she lit each cigarette
from the last and stored the pack
deep in a breast pocket.
As her pale lips grew tight about
each word in praise of work and abstinence
- tired but polite,
three hours before midnight,
I remembered an old and younger friend -
holding a room in the spell of her talk,
a lover in one arm, a bottle in the other -
drunk at dawn...and laughing.

It Has Rained All Night While We Slept

Women have given birth
in fields
while we slept.
While we slept
women have given birth.

The mountains are huge.
A wall of iron around my heart.
The lakes, bitter black pools.
Women have drowned
in water, shallow as a basin.
Women have drowned their babies
in water no deeper
than a pool or basin
while we slept.

It has rained all night.
We wake to find it
heavy as snowfall on the window
the fields drenched with it
the earth, the stones, the leaves.
It has gouged streams
glittering
along the mountain side.

And while we slept
somewhere else -
a child has died.
Somewhere else
while we sleep
some woman's child dies
every hour
that we sleep.

Somewhere else
the split, yellow earth
littered with their bodies
dark skin, white bones
that lie quiet
as snow lies in the ruined fields.
Every hour dying
while we sleep
here,
the rain falling.
We have grown used to it.
We do not hear
the rain falling.

We know them well -
these women and their children
- or their faces.
We have grown used to them.
They follow us about
from billboards
buses

and dentists' waiting rooms -
framed in magazines
and television sets.
Eyes beautiful and blank.
Bellies - oh, bellies
big and taut
as a cow's udder.
Their hands reaching
open mouthed
to no one in particular.

All night
the rain has fallen
covering our sleep like snow.
And somewhere -
oh, somewhere out of camera -
the eyes that would not
turn from us
have closed at last.
The sweet
pitiless eyes
have shut,
disturbing
for a moment -
while we slept -

the blow-flies.

An Ungrammatical Poem

And you,
the rain on our skin,
the sun beating,
you - sweet, guileful sister
of pleasure,
you said in my ear

my mind turning
my body in your hands
turning,
you said,
say my name
when you come

and I did
say it,
your name
say it as well
as I could,
coming so many times

which is perhaps why
rain beating, sun on the skin
I say it still sometimes,
your name, when I come
so long after
you went.

Because She Carried Flowers

Because she carried flowers:
Lilac and wild red poppies
When first she came to my bed,
I loved her.

Because she carried flowers:
Marigold and lilies
To another woman's bed,
I left her.

When You're Asleep

I'm worn out with you.

All day long
fetching and carrying
upstairs and downstairs
my back broken
picking up after you
forever under my feet.

Upstairs   downstairs
your questions trailing me
never quiet for two
minutes together -

How old were you the year that we went...?
Do you remember the time
somebody said ...?
Wasn't it grand the first
summer we saw ...?
Were you born yet
the last winter your father and I ...?
Just let me tell you once more -
I know I've told you already ...

I'm worn out with you.

But for you these are festival
days;
days you can talk
all day long

out loud for a change
morning to night,
banqueting
because I'm here
to listen.

As the hours journey
from one meal to another
I hear my voice give out
an old litany:
Eat up now
stop talking
your food will be cold.
Mind the stairs
don't hurry ... you'll fall ...

Fasten your buttons
put on your slippers
watch where you're going
come on now - we're late ...
wash yourself quickly
get into bed
it's all hours already.
Pull up your covers ...
Yes -
I'll leave the door open ...

At last you're quiet
at last it's over -
all over again
until tomorrow
and I'm too tired
to kiss you or say goodnight.

Free -
I can go downstairs
read a book
or watch television.

I'm worn out with you.

Last of all
I look in
to see if you're sleeping -
your head sunk in the pillows
so still and so small ...
when did it grow so small?
I draw close
breath held
to catch yours -
and yes,
there it is -
softly, your mouth
almost smiling
the cat curled at your shoulder.

And I'm returned
thirty years or more
when I would call out
at night
as you closed the door
to hold you there
one moment longer.
Do you love me still?
I'd sing;
and back came the same answer
always -
When you're asleep!

II

from 'Kindling'

After Long Silence

We regard each other
awkwardly, speechless
we who have so much
to unsay
to forget or at least forgive.

And then
in unconscious diplomacy,
with that old grace
that so often came
between you and your consequences

You stretch your hand
to mine
and some ember of the me
that I was to you,
rekindles
and in silence,
recovers the power of
speech.

Blood Relations

Leaving
she bends to kiss you
slowly on each cheek,
drawing closer to let slip
a few last words
in your foreign tongue
and I, discreet,
embarrassed to be the chosen
the one who stays,
lower my eyes and pretend indifference
granting her one last intimacy.

Can you blame me then
if I forget,
that it is only your mother
saying goodbye after morning coffee
whose eyes as they acknowledge mine
are brilliant with shamed jealousy?

Woman in a Normandy Field

She stood alone
under a grey sky's impassive discipline,
dark earth stretched about her beyond sight
  its raw furrows gaping.
Turning full circle she surveyed a year's work
  laid out like a cloth before her.
Then slowly her knees bent to ground once more
  and with deliberate hands
she began the season's first task.

America

They had boasted it
as something special, an ancient house
in the European style.
As I entered the old rooms and felt
their years cluster about me
I was at peace for the first time.
I gazed out the dark windows, sheltered
by the knowledge that I was just one
of so many others, to have watched these
great trees do battle with the wind

Or heard their leaves break and fall
in an autumn dusk.
And I understood then the loneliness
that I feel in this brash new country,
where everything is being done
as though never before.
Where there are no other presences
to keep me company,
no guiding hand in shadow at an open
door. No echo beneath our talk

Of those other inhabitants
- the half-seen face in the glass
- the sigh of their lost conversation,
reminding me that we are not alone
and need not struggle so anxiously
always to be first or last.
I miss those presences, quiet about me.
Here in this young country it seems
the air is too thin to fill lungs
grown rich with the breath of ghosts.

Mirrors

At the foot of your garden
The sea plunges in its narrow bed.
Stilled by its clamour you stand,

Peonies and lupin that he planted
The year of his death, each summer
Recover their place about you. You

Have grown old in their light. You
Have watched your children go from
You and said no word to halt them. You

Have friends and books - money enough
A good neighbour to one side - six
Grandchildren. But your daughters will

Never marry now and you will never
See your eyes shine from the faces of
Their daughters. This one regret

You hold in silence, for you have other
Windows to the world, through which you
Glimpse a life and loves not spoken of

In well curtained drawingrooms. I
Walk from you with my woman lover
Down the smooth flower lined path,

Your smile follows me to the gate and
No stranger passing could tell what
Dark pleasures are mirrored in your eyes.

Spring

The coming of Spring
has quickened my ears,
and I hear faint sounds
that the snow of winter
muffled; the cry of sea birds
on the coast,
and the harshness that now
edges your voice.

Night

I remember your neck, its strength
and the sweetness of the skin at you throat.
I remember your hair, long, in our way
drawing it back from my mouth.
How my hands slid the low plain of your back
thrown by the sudden flaunt of your loins.
I remember your voice, the first low break
and at last the long flight
loosing us to darkness.
And your lips along my shoulder,
more sure, even than I had imagined -
how I guarded their track.

I ask you then what am I to do with all these
memories
heavy and full?
Hold them, quiet, between my two hands,
as I would if I could again
your hard breasts?

Autumn

I wish I had never seen
that smile you sent
over your lover's shoulder
to another woman's eyes,
did you have to remind me tonight
how soon the leaves fall
in this part of the country?

Photographs

On a bare boned pram a young seagull stood,
grey water slipped between rocks and tin cans
dribbling a green froth along its flanks, while
    dun coloured ducks swam among the debris
    salvaging bread from plastic wrappers.
Then I saw it - drifting on the slow current, a
woman's arm naked in the thin sunlight, and
at the water's edge, a black stockinged thigh
    half buried in mud and silt.
I looked about and saw

That rocks and sand were littered
with broken bits of flesh,
breasts and hips in white lace underwear,
    smooth brown torsos strewn idly
    among empty bottles and paper bags.
One face stared up
with a hideous lipsticked grin,
ripped from its shoulders
    yet still determined to please.
Some boys behind me shouted -

'Hey lads look at the dirty photos!' And they
were just that, to any normal eye, just that,
photographs - only pictures.
    Blow-ups from some glossy porno magazine
    discarded in shame or boredom
to float dismembered on the river
exposed to every vacant glance.
With a whoop and snigger
    the boys raced towards the shore but
 a shout of rage that shocked my ears

Stalled them in their tracks - and I climbed past
them to the bank's wet sand, where looking
at the first stained face, some helpless,
   protective urge, made me kneel to gather up
   the sodden bits and pieces of women, who they say,
had long since lost the right to care
who looked or touched. Later, regaining the road
I bound them tight in old newspaper
   struck a match and set them flaming
blue green into the sunlight.

Words Without Echo

Come then
forget that you saw it
forget that I said it,
forget the cold truths
that have come between us like glass.

Forgive the body
that has such different things to say
and only one way to say them.
Forget the old luxuries:
words without echo
eyes with no reflection.

Come then
- many flowers blossom on one stem
kiss me,
and I will not ask
why you close your eyes.

Before the Tide

A slow sea,
a long clear stretch of sand.
The usual things - glazed wood and stone,
seaweed stacked in a glistening breakwater.
Far down, near the harbour
a white dog barking at a wave.

Then - full in the sun
as if laid out to dry,
the wings of some great sea
bird - something like a cormorant
spread wide on a granite rock.
Drawing near
I see the head is twisted back
- startled by a sudden noise?

Its beak plunged between smooth
feathers - black with a sheen of purple.
At the belly a grey foot dangles
like a twig snapped in its fall.
One eye is sealed with mud,
the other staring upwards
as if the sky had frozen in it.

Overhead a hundred gulls scream
above a movement in the air,
gliding and buffeting
- not one falling.

In the fields beyond
swifts dart and butterfly
a horse and foal stand, yellow flowers
blown about their hooves.

A low gust rifles
the sand
snatches a tail feather
throws it across stones to sea.

And I stare down
at this unmoving thing
that will not flinch from wind
or human eye.
Fixed and soundless, before the tide
the only creature of its kind
as if it were
an unusual thing
to die.

Night Protest

We stood outside that prison wall,
The slow rain speared by barbed wire,
Stood outside and called your name.
Called against the dark and our own dread
In the shadow of that grey stone mass,
Where each square foot of twilight
Is held behind bars.
Then through the clouded air something

Fluttered white - a strip of sheet
Or handkerchief
Making its own small peace there
By reaching out to us.
And was it your voice that broke clear?
Two hundred stood in silence but
It did not come again.
Later a cell light flashed

Once - twice - a signal surely
Or just some careless warder?
So we sang for you the old battle songs
For you who had so often stood
On both sides of this wall,
And someone set a placard burning
Sparking a passage for our voices,
And I wanted to call *'She's still*

Carrying a torch for your Marie.'
Nell cried the last message *'We'll be*
Seeing you soon again but we have
To go home for our dinners now.'
And I thought of yours that day,
Each day - the oiled tea, damp bread,
The egg and sausage floating
On a tin plate.

And I tried not to think of those other
Abuses - the little things that cripple:
The drooling eye at the peep-hole
And two sanitary towels - per woman
- Per month.
And how many others inside that fortress
Strained to hear their own name spoken?
How many others forgotten

Unknown
In for a pound of butter
Or for servicing some man in a car.
So we sang for them too
'Oh sisters don't you weep, don't you
Moan' and maybe they knew.
We left one by one, some still calling
A name or a joke

Moving slowly for your sake
But wanting to run from the damp
Infectious air of that place.
And the 'Branch' men sullen in their
Cars, watched us pass stiff eyed
The sense beginning to grip at last,
That they'd more than one
Brazen bitch - banging the bars.

Friendship

Although we had talked all night,
about rejection, hurt
and the bitterness of those
we had once most trusted,
lying in your arms, in a warm bed,
rummaging through our injuries
like two old drunken women on a bench,

It no longer mattered at all
- none of it.
Breast against breast
desiring nothing more than sleep,
loss was a once sharp blade
that had cut me loose
for this friendship.

House in Winter

In a cold room
dawn light stirs on skin.
Wind sucks at the roof beams,
lip to bone we rekindle
the old track of heat along the nerves.
From hand to widening eye
the spark climbs
the taut rope of your spine.
Ribs crack like tinder.

Below us
someone moves about the empty house.
Our cupped hands hold the flame
our mouths suckle it.
Footsteps mount the stairs
shudder through our breathing.
Higher and higher - they come
stumble past the door
and quicken -

My hands fly loose
your eyes catch fire.
From heart and lungs and belly
breath sings -
the air shatters
in spears of ringing crystal
blue and gold and silver.

Somewhere below
a door slams shut
returning us.
Silence seeps like snow
about the roof and walls.
But listen -

at the window
we have startled a yellow wasp
from winter.
With a fevered hum
it climbs the chill glass
beating its way to summer.

In a cold room
we reach slowly
and draw the fallen covers
up from our feet.

ABOUT THE AUTHOR

Mary Dorcey was born and raised in Co. Dublin, Ireland, and has lived in France, Spain, England, America and Japan.

She has been active in the Women's Movement since 1972 and was a founder member of Irish Women United and the Irish Gay Rights movement.

Her collection of short stories, 'A Noise from the Woodshed', won the Rooney Prize for Literature in 1991. It was chosen as one of the Top Twenty Titles for Feminist Book Fortnight in Britain in that year.

Her first collection of poetry, 'Kindling' (Onlywomen Press) was published in Britain in 1982.

A novella, 'Scarlett O'Hara' was published in the collection 'In and Out of Time' (Onlywomen Press, 1990).

Her collection of poetry, 'Moving into the Space Cleared by Our Mothers', was published by Salmon in 1991 and is being taught at the Irish Studies Course at Yale University.

Her poetry and stories have been anthologised in numerous collections, ranging from 'Bread and Roses' (Virago Press, 1984), to 'New Angles' (Oxford University Press, 1990), most recently, 'The State of the Art Modern Irish Short Stories' editor David Marcus, (Sceptre, 1993), 'Virgins and Hyacinths', editor Caroline Walshe, (Attic Press, 1993), 'The Picador Collection of Modern Irish Fiction' editor Dermot Bolger, (Picador, 1993), 'Six Soho Square' editor Colm Toibin, (Bloomsbury, 1993), 'Irish Love Stories' editor David Marcus, (Sceptre, 1994), 'Ireland's Women: Writings Past and Present', editor Brendan Kennelly, (Kyle Cathie Limited, 1994).

A story, 'The Lift Home' was published in *The Irish Times* Summer Fiction series (1990).

Her story 'The Husband' was published in Image magazine, 1993.

Her poem 'Night' is represented in 'The Great Book of Ireland'.

Her work is taught on Irish Studies and Women's Studies courses at universities in Ireland, Britain, Canada and America. Her poetry has been performed on stage, radio and television (RTE and Channel 4).

In 1991 she was awarded an Arts Council Bursary for Literature.

Her poetry has been dramatised in stage productions in Ireland and Britain – 'Sunnyside Plucked' and 'In the Pink', which toured Europe and Australia.

She has led creative writing workshops in Ireland and England since 1982 and has been a guest lecturer at all Irish universities and has given talks on women's writing and politics in numerous public fora. She has been a guest speaker at each International Feminist Book Fair since 1982 in London, Barcelona, Oslo and Amsterdam.

Mary Dorcey is currently at work on a play 'The Interrogation of an Ordinary Woman' and a new collection of short stories. Her first novel, 'A Biography of Desire' will be published in Autumn 1994. She lives in Co. Wicklow.